Write About Math!

More than 200 Creative Prompts to Develop Essential Math Skills

by

Richard S. Piccirilli, Ph.D.

SCHOLASTIC PROFESSIONAL BOOKS

New York ◆ Toronto ◆ London ◆ Auckland ◆ Sydney

Dedication

This book is dedicated to the Three Pics plus Two who are the loves of my life and to the memory of Mr. Paul Hayden, former Assistant Superintendent for Instruction for the Penfield Central School District, whose faith in me started me on a thirty-year career in mathematics education.

Acknowledgments

To my editors Virginia Dooley and Terry Cooper—thank you for your encouragement. A generous thank you is extended to Mark and Linda Decker for typing the manuscript.

Cover design by Vincent Ceci
Interior design by Jo-Ann Rosiello
Cover illustrations by Rick Brown
Interior illustrations by Rick Brown

ISBN 0-590-67476-5

Table of Contents

Introduction

Communicating mathematics through writing is considered so important by the National Council of Teachers of Mathematics that NCTM has established learning to *communicate mathematically* among its five important goals for mathematics instruction.

Can everyone really write about math? Of course they can if the content of their writing is familiar to them. Young children study math in school and use it in their daily lives. The content of their math writing should be a natural outgrowth of their rich school and life experiences with math.

The purpose of this book is to get students to write about mathematics whether in journals, logs, diaries, notes, and letters, or through music, poetry, literature, or bumper stickers! Students can write about math during math class, Language Arts time, or for homework. This book should help to get the class started by providing prompts, suggesting fertile areas for writing math, or stimulating you, *the teacher*, to develop your own meaningful topics for writing math.

Write About Math! provides a variety of ways to increase students' conceptual knowledge of mathematics through writing. Additionally, related reading, speaking, and listening activities are an outgrowth of writing math. The ideas in this book are intended to present various topics that cross age and grade levels of student writers.

The math ideas may be presented to the class, or assigned to cooperative learning groups or individuals. Drawings and/or illustrations should be encouraged to help clarify writing. Sharing is encouraged but in some cases, writers may want to keep their ideas and feelings private. Writing should be logical and organized. Writers should feel good about their writing. The mechanics of good writing, such as spelling, complete sentences, punctuation, and capitalization should also be encouraged but not forced to the detriment of the students' ideas. Both teachers and students are encouraged to do some writing every day.

Using writing to learn mathematics, or using mathematics to learn about writing and thinking is a useful tool for teachers.

Write About Math! encourages different types of writing. Children are asked to do *narrative writing*, where students write stories, and word problems, explain social uses of mathematics, or report on biographies of mathematicians or everyday people who use math. The second type deals with *descriptive writing*. Here student writers describe mathematical events, or algorithms. They also may write about how numbers behave, or share discoveries they have made. The third type deals with expository writing. Here the topics encourage the students to express their feelings, personal insights, difficulties, needs, perceptions, or misconceptions. They may seek help here or give advice to others about their personal thoughts about mathematics.

Hopefully, you and your students will find the topics interesting to write about, talk about, or debate. In the process, students will learn more mathematics, understand it better, and will enjoy it even more.

Why Write Math?

Students need to write math because it enables them to learn more math, and to integrate it into their lives. Writing math provides the learner with added opportunities to think, write, and reflect on mathematics and opportunities for students to describe their math feelings. Additionally, writing math helps students to:

- ▶ reveal the nature of their thinking
- ▶ clarify and consolidate new information
- ▶ discover misconceptions
- ▶ accomplish Language Arts goals in writing, listening, reading, and speaking

How to Use This Book

There are some overlaps among the three chapters in this book, but the intent is to present a sequence that is meaningful to teachers.

The first chapter deals with writing about mathematics as it relates to the student, the math class, the math teacher, and math content. Numerous math topics are presented here for writing.

The second chapter deals with writing about mathematics as it relates to the students' use of math outside of school. The general topics presented are associated with spending, sports, games, family, and opinions.

The third chapter deals with writing about mathematics in the context of a Language Arts class. Here, math is used as content for researching and writing stories, reports, letters, critiques, and reviews.

Getting Started

To maximize the use of this book, the reader is encouraged to first skim the material to gain familiarity with the content and organization, and next to read the book to find ideas that are appropriate for the user's class.

Teachers are encouraged to begin in a lighthearted vein, where children might be creating math bumper stickers (page 56), math quotes for T-shirts (page 57), or a math graffiti board (page 56). The idea is to have students develop a sense that math is a very fertile area about which to write. Next, many teachers have found that a transition into the more traditional type of writing is to ask students what they think or feel or know about a math topic that is of interest to them.
These can include responding to such questions as, "Tell what you know about...."
or "How do you think you're doing in math?" or "Write five test items," or
"Write a note to the teacher..."Once writing math has become a common event, teachers should find the ideas presented here to be a springboard into different math topics and different types of writing. Finally, the book will provide numerous opportunities to read, speak, listen, and write math, thus helping students to communicate mathematically.

Other Suggestions

Date journals, diaries, logs, assignments. This allows students to put their written work in chronological order so that they can look for trends or changes in their attitude and/or math progress.

Let students select topics sometimes. Students will have a greater investment in their work.

Teachers should assign topics sometimes. By selecting writing topics, teachers can focus writing math activities on specific curriculum goals.

Make writing math typical class work, not an add-on.
Students will view the work as a necessary part of their growth in learning math.

Use Language Arts and math time to write about math.

The teacher who uses math or Language Arts time to write about math is serving curriculum goals from both curriculum areas.

Respond to student writing with encouraging comments.

Encouraging comments help students feel that you, the teacher, feel that what the student writes is important, and they will encourage more thinking and reflection.

Provide opportunities for students to share with the class or with an individual student or small groups of students.

Students will learn math ideas and writing styles from other students.

Encourage drawings and using colored pencils for lively illustrations.
Creating visuals may be a good outlet for artistic and non-artistic students.

Provide a risk-free environment.
Students will be honest in their writing math if they feel teachers and listeners will not be critical.

When appropriate, model an activity.
Students will find it interesting to hear and see what the teacher would do with a particular written math assignment.

With student permission, duplicate or make transparencies of student work to share with the class.
This can not only add variety and interest to writing math time, but can help students win acclaim for their ideas and work.

Provide opportunities for students to reread their written work after several weeks or months have elapsed.
Students will be surprised at how much they have learned, matured, improved, or changed.

Encourage the use of proper writing mechanics.
Help students realize how correct mechanics give a clearer understanding of ideas, greater credibility to the author, and provide a courtesy to the reader so that ideas are not obscured by writing errors. Work out the mechanics <u>after</u> the writing math activity.

Math Class

Students learn much of what they know about math in math class. It is here where concepts are explored, where hypotheses are formulated and tested, where questions are asked and answered, where literature is explored, and where students interact with other math students, their teachers, and with math content. Ideas as well as feelings are developed here. It is in math class that writing math benefits the student by providing opportunities to learn more. For the teacher, much feedback is gained by reading student writing. Not only is it an assessment tool for students, but it also provides the math teacher with feedback about instructional decisions for the math student and the math class.

The chapter starts with students writing about themselves, classmates, and teachers. Next, they are led into a variety of math content from math vocabulary to writing about problem solving.

Writing About Math Class

With whom would you like to work as a math partner? Why?

Write an ad for a math partner that begins: "I'm looking for a math partner. I prefer someone who is..."

Tell how you feel about working in a cooperative group.

Do you prefer working alone or with a math partner? Tell why.

Here are some things you may or may not know about my math group.

What things did you like about working in a math group? What did you dislike?

In your group, who worked the most to get the assignment done? Explain what that person did.

What qualities make the head of your math group a leader?

With whom in the class would you like to work with as a math partner? Tell why.

How is math similar to other school subjects?

How many students are in your math class? How many are boys? Girls?

List the names, addresses, phone numbers, and birthdays of your friends.

What did you do in math class today?

What ideas or concepts did you understand in today's math lesson? What didn't you understand?

Finish any one of these sentences:

Today I learned...

I liked...

Tomorrow the class will...

I was surprised that...

Now I know that...

The most important thing to remember about today's math lesson is...

What do you think your teacher was trying to teach in math today?

What did you learn in math today that you did not know before?

How and when might you use the math that you learned today?

What did you learn in math this week?

Write a letter to a student who will be entering your class next week. Describe what you enjoy most about your math class. What suggestions would you make to improve the class?

Make up three questions for your next math test.

What important points do you want to remember for the upcoming test?

Tell how you studied for the math test.

How do some of your friends feel about math?

A friend says, "Well, I don't think we need to know so much math!" What is your reaction to that?

Describe the time you helped someone with his or her math homework.

What goals should you set for yourself in math?

Put an "X" in the box that expresses your feelings about math.

❑ Confusing

❑ Understandable

Explain why you put the "X" where you did.

What are your math goals for the year?

Describe how math is similar to other school subjects. How is it different?

What are your math goals for next week?

Is math easy or difficult for you?

What's the most difficult thing for you to do in math?

How often do you share math ideas and information with the rest of the class?

Put an "X" in the box that indicates how much of a risk-taker you are.

❏ Risk-taker

❏ Not a risk-taker

Explain why you put the "X" where you did.

Are you ever careless when you're doing your math homework? Explain your answer.

What can you do to make fewer mistakes in math?

Why should you check your work?

What do you do when you need help with your math homework?

Whom do you turn to when you have difficulties with your math homework? Why that person?

Complete the following sentence: "When I have math homework I..."

Describe when and where you do your math homework.

On the back of your math homework paper, write the answer to one or more of the following questions:

1. **What did you think of the assignment?**

2. **Which problem was the most difficult?**

3. **Did you learn anything new?**

4. **What questions do you still have?**

What is the one thing about math that you like best?

What math activities have you found interesting?

Choose a sample of your best work. Write on the back of the paper why you selected this as a sample of your best work.

What is the one thing about math that you like least?

What math questions do you have that you would like answered?

How would you like to be graded in math?

Write a letter to your teacher comparing your progress in math this year to your progress last year.

Write a note to your teacher suggesting ways students could earn extra credit in math.

Meet with your math teacher to discuss your progress this year. Then write a description of the meeting. Remember to mention whether you or your math teacher need to meet again. Finally, give the description to your teacher.

If there were 25 students in your math class, where would you rank? Use a number. Why would you rank yourself this way?

Why would you want to know your grade average in a subject?

If your grade average is low in math, how can you improve it?

Explain in a note to an absent classmate what was done in math class today.

Write a letter to inform someone (teacher, parent, friend) of your progress in math. You might want to mention what you have been doing to help it along.

Write a letter to your last year's teacher, telling how you are doing in math. Mention if there is anything you studied last year that you learned more about this year.

Is there a number that you see more frequently than others? What number is it and where have you seen it?

How do you use math when telling time?

Tell about your school day from the time you wake up in the morning until the time you go to bed. Give the time you do each activity.

Provide your vital statistics: height, weight, waist size, hand size, shoe size, etc...

Write about the metric you! Tell in metric units:
• height • hand size • weight
• waist size • shoe size

List five choices—by writing first, second, third, etc.—of places you want to visit.

How do you use a computer to study math?

Writing About the Math Teacher

Write a note to your teacher describing your thoughts and feelings about math homework.

If you could tell your teacher anything about your math class, what would it be?

Make a list of math questions you want your teacher to answer. (The teacher chooses the questions, answers them, and has students write the answers in their journal.)

What advice would you give to your math teacher?

How does your teacher use math in school everyday?

Suppose the teacher gives you all the answers to your math homework. How do you think he or she would expect you to use them?

How could your math class earn money for a trip to Washington, D.C.?

Write a note to your teacher describing your ideas for decorating the classroom with a math theme.

Invent a math game and give it to your teacher with a note asking if the game could be played in class.

Interview a math teacher to find out whether he or she enjoys teaching math.

What math materials would you like to see your teacher order?

Math Vocabulary

Write a list of math words. Then arrange the words so that the first letter of each one forms another math word or topic. For example:

Geometric **D**igits **M**athematics
Euclid **A**rranging **A**ccurate
Obtuse **T**ally **T**riangles
Measuring **A**nswers **H**ypotenuse
Easy
Trapezoid **A**ddend
Rhombus **D**igits
Yes! ! **D**ecimals

What others can you make up?

• •

How is pi different from pie?
Write a sentence using both words.

Explain what these numbers mean and how we use them.

K-9	H_2O
9 to 5	0°C
1040	WD40
911	seven-eleven
98.6°	4 bits
409	1180am

Add three more numbers to the above list.

Make a list of prefixes often found in math.
Example:

**bi means 2
tri means 3
quad means 4
equi means equal**

Make words using these prefixes. Select one of your words and then write a sentence using it.

Write a separate sentence for each word or phrase below:

**...just a minute
...whenever
...once upon a time
...any time now
...at no time whatsoever
...sooner or later
...before long
...in a second**

Write three other phrases that indicate time and include each one in a sentence.

What is math?

What does *infinity* mean to you? Write a few examples that show infinity.

How do you define _____?
(You can fill in the blank space for your class.)

A friend of mine can't seem to remember that 7 x 9 = 63. What would you tell him so that he can easily remember it?

A digit not only is a numeral, but it is also a finger. How do you think the word meaning finger also came to mean numeral?

"I have time on my hands!" one man said to another. What do you suppose he meant?

Use the words pi, diameter, and circumference in a sentence.

Use the words pi, radius, and area in a sentence.

What is a palindrome?

Explain how you would find the palindrome for 38.

Make a list of 10 words that are palindromes. Example: Mom, wow, Bob, etc. Write a sentence where every word is a palindrome.

What is a tessellation? Explain with words and a drawing.

Some math words have more than one meaning. Read the following examples:

What's your *angle*?
Do you *measure* up to the task?
My injured *foot* required two stitches.

Write sentences using the following math words. Remember to use each word in a context other than for math.

- **pattern**
- **remainder**
- **number**
- **sphere**
- **yard**
- **rounding**
- **pound**
- **square**
- **point**

List five other words that have the same math beginnings as those given below.

bi-
biplane
bisect

multi-
multiple
multifaceted

tri-
triangle
tricycle

sum-
summary
summation

quad-
quadruplets
quadrilateral

Choose one word from each group and write a sentence for each word.

What do you know about _____?
(You can suggest a word that is the name of a math topic to be studied.)

Manipulatives

What did you discover when you were working with math manipulatives?

Tell why a particular math manipulative is your favorite.

Get a handful of buttons. Describe four different categories into which you could put each one. What did you do with buttons that didn't fit into any of the categories?

How would you use a number line?

What characteristics do $1, $2, $5, $10, $20, $50, and $100 bills share in common?

Annette weighs herself and her dog, Basil, whom she holds in her arms. Then she weighs just herself. Explain how you could figure out how much Basil weighs.

Patterns

Examine a hundred chart. Write about the different patterns that you notice.

What number sentences can you write for 18? List the different sentences. Put similar number sentences together. Write what you noticed.

In math you often see patterns. Explain what a pattern is and provide an example of one.

Write about the patterns you see in the nine table below.

$$0 \times 9 = 0$$
$$1 \times 9 = 9$$
$$2 \times 9 = 18$$
$$3 \times 9 = 27$$
$$4 \times 9 = 36$$
$$5 \times 9 = 45$$
$$6 \times 9 = 54$$
$$7 \times 9 = 63$$
$$8 \times 9 = 72$$
$$9 \times 9 = 81$$
$$10 \times 9 = 90$$

What patterns do you see?

Examine a calendar. Then, write what you notice about it. What patterns do you see?

Carl Gauss could add all the 100 numbers on the 100 board in his head in less than one minute. How did he do it?

Explain how you would figure out the next three numbers in the pattern consisting of **1, 1, 2, 3, 5, 8, 13....**

Explain a strategy, or short-cut, for learning addition, subtraction, multiplication, or division by the number 9.

How does knowing that 36 ÷ 9 = 4 help you to figure out the answer to 3600 ÷ 900?

Use a calculator to change 1/9 to a decimal. Now change 2/9 to a decimal. What would you predict is the decimal value for 8/9? Why? Check on your calculator. Are you right?

Use a calculator to change the fractions below to decimals:

1/11 or 1 ÷ 11 =
2/11 or 2 ÷ 11 =

Now write the rest of the pattern without using the calculator. How were you able to come up with the pattern?

Which is larger, 1/4 or 1/2 ? Write to a friend and tell him or her how you know which fraction is larger.

It may be difficult for some students to understand that 3/4 and 6/8 have the same value. Explain how 3/4 could equal 6/8. Include in your explanation the number and size of the pieces and how they relate to each other.

Number Theory

Look at the diagram below. Then list the members of each set. Describe each set in a sentence. Explain what the different sets have in common.

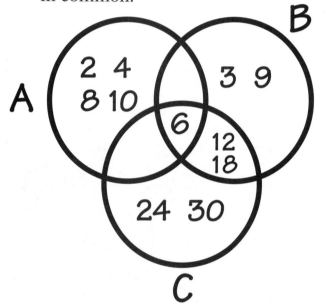

How did the Egyptians count?

Book Link

After reading *Zero: Is It Something? Is It Nothing* by Claudia Zaslavsky, give examples when zero is something and when zero is nothing.

How did the Romans count?

How is zero used?

How can you recognize an odd number? An even number?

Why is the expression $2x + 1$ an odd number?

Describe as many different ways as possible to show whether 17 is an odd or an even number.

What happens when you add two even numbers together? How about two odd numbers? How about an odd number and an even number? How about two odd numbers and one even number?

How do you think the number five developed?

Explain how you think the numbers 10 and 20 developed.

A famous Hollywood star, Greta Garbo, once said that 10 not only is her lucky number, but that she also enjoys the number 10 in math. Why would she enjoy the number 10 in math?

Other than the number 2, why can't a prime number be even?

What happens when you multiply a prime number by a prime number?

Why is 51 not a prime number?

What is an abundant number? A deficient number? A perfect number? A composite number?

Two numbers were talking. One number said, "Children like me better than they like you." The two numbers arguing were 12 and 13. What do you think each number said in order to prove it was right?

Describe the numbers between 1 and 2. Hint: Think about fractions and/or decimals.

Todd made a machine filled with numbers. It could add, subtract, multiply, or divide. One day Todd put in the number 4 and out came the number 400. What do you think the machine did to the 4?

How do you know if a number is divisible by 2? 3? 6? or 9?

Here's a question that appeared on a math test. Explain how you could choose the correct answer almost immediately. What's the answer to:

37 x 468?

1. 17,613

2. 17,163

3. 17,316

4. 17,631

Why can you do this problem in your head?

386 x 11 x 167 x 0 x 2 x 3 =

Use your calculator to multiply
3 x 37,037.

Now try 6 x 37,037.
What will you get when you
multiply 9 x 37,037?
12 x 37,037?
Explain why you can predict
777,777 for 21 x 37,037.

This is called a magic square. Why?

4	9	2
3	5	7
8	1	6

Book Link

After reading
The King's Chessboard
by David Birch, describe how the wise man was able to get so much rice from the king.

Explain Marianne's math observation. "In order to divide by a decimal," she said, "you make changes and you end up dividing by a whole number."

Think of a way you can help a friend remember that > means greater than, and that < means less than.

Your spelling test grades were 80%, 90%, and 70%. Your average in spelling is 80%. Explain what that means.

How would you explain the distributive property to a friend?

Geometry

What does geometry mean to you?

Try answering the following riddle:
  I have a shape.
  It has one more side than a triangle.
  It has 4 right angles.
  All the sides are equal.
  Who am l?
  Can you draw me?

Choose a shape to write your own riddle:

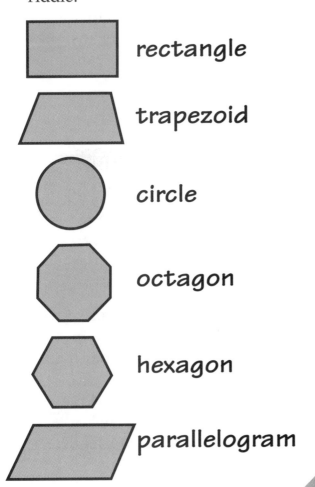

rectangle

trapezoid

circle

octagon

hexagon

parallelogram

Which of the following shapes does not belong and why: Square, trapezoid, rectangle, and triangle? Make up your own questions similar to this one.

Which shape do you prefer: triangle, circle, rectangle, diamond, or square? Explain why. What objects do these shapes remind you of?

All squares are rectangles, but not all rectangles are squares. How come?

Describe at least four different ways you can cut a square in half.

Describe a rhombus.

rhombus

Tell how a radius and a diameter are related.

Explain why the human body is considered symmetrical.

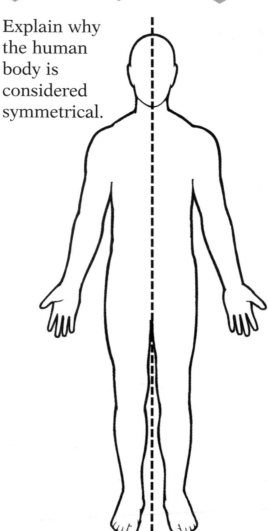

List ten things you can see immediately that have circles in them.

Ken says all circles are congruent. Annette says all circles are similar. Explain who is right.

If a triangle is obtuse, what do you know about the size of each of the three angles? What do you know about the largest angle and the other two angles?

Figure out how many blocks are in the drawing. How did you arrive at that number?

What's the difference between square feet and cubic feet?

Which drawing(s) would fold up into a box. How do you know?

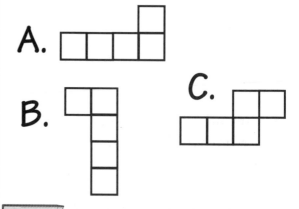

A.

B.

C.

Book Link

After reading
A Cloak for the Dreamer
by Aileen Friedman,
describe how you would cut
a circle into a hexagon.

Measurement

Imagine that you are one centimeter tall. Describe some interesting experiences you might have had.

Kenneth tells his dad that if you were to measure a person's height, your answer would never be completely accurate. Explain what he meant.

Why are all 12-inch rulers the same size? What would happen if they weren't?

What are some different ways of measuring time?

Why is it helpful to understand time zones?

What math is involved if you were making a box 2 feet, by 2 feet, by 2 feet?

How is a thermometer like a number line?

Describe the last trip you made with your family. Where were you headed? What kinds of road signs did you see?

Explain how you can figure out the distance between your home and a distant place you want to visit.

Book Link

After reading
The Librarian Who Measured the Earth
by Kathryn Lasky,
tell what information Eratosthenes needed to measure the circumference of the earth.

Read the humorous book
Counting on Frank
by Rod Clement,
What are some funny things that the boy tried to measure?

Find out how many miles it is from your hometown to a place you would like to visit. Explain why it is worth traveling all that distance.

Statistics and Probability

Explain why surveys are used.

Make a survey of the number of people in your class who wear glasses.

Make a survey of the number of classmates who wear digital watches and the number who wear regular watches. What are your findings?

Tell whether you think the game below is fair. Here's how to play:

1. The winner is the one who earns the most points after 5 minutes of play. Take turns spinning.

2. The first player earns points by landing on 1.
3. The second player earns points by landing on 2. Is the game fair? Why? How could you make it fair?

Measure the height of five friends. Then, for each person, measure the distance from the floor to his or her waist. Make a fraction using the two distances. Total height should go on the bottom. Finally, divide the numerator by the denominator using a calculator. What do you notice about your answers?

Survey the students in your class. Look for any one or a combination of the following:

The number of students who:

1. wear T-shirts versus those who don't

2. have footwear with laces versus those without

3. wear sneakers versus those without sneakers

4. blond hair versus those without blond hair

5. wear jeans versus those without jeans

What conclusions can you draw from your data?

What factors do you consider when predicting tomorrow's weather?

What is the weather report for tomorrow? Include the following information:

▶ **high and low temperature**
▶ **wind speed**
▶ **dew point**
▶ **amount of precipitation**
▶ **air pressure**

Cut out a graph from a newspaper or magazine. Write five questions that the graph could answer.

Make a pie graph that shows how you spend your allowance money. Tell why you spend your allowance the way you do.

Make a list of the kinds and amount of food you eat in one day. How many calories do you consume in total? Comment on foods you like and foods you dislike but eat anyway.

How many letters do you have in your name?
▶ Which letter appears most frequently?
▶ Which letter appears only once?
▶ Which letters are vowels?
▶ How many letters are consonants?
Make a chart of all this information.

Cut out a chart from a newspaper or magazine, or reproduce one from your social studies textbook. Write five questions that are answered by the chart.

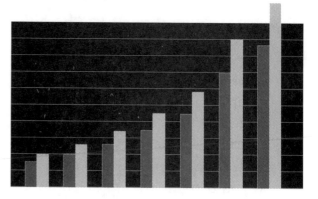

Make a survey of the number of phones, bathrooms, bedrooms, chairs, windows, and clocks in your home. Present the results in a chart.

Record the number of completed school days and the number of days until the end of the school year. Put this information on a chart so that the numbers can easily be changed daily.

Calculators

The "4" key on your calculator is broken. Explain how you would add 3454 + 4621.

Make up similar examples for other operations. For example, the number "3" key is broken. How would you multiply 395 x 12?

Explain what the √ key on a calculator does.

Explain how to use the M (memory) button on a calculator.

Explain how to use the % button on a calculator.

When was the last time you used a calculator? What did you use it for?

Mental Math

Describe two different ways of scoring 150 points on a dartboard by using only 3 darts.

List the different ways you can score 100 points by using 4 darts. You can hit the same number more than once. Explain how you arrived at your answer.

Explain how you can figure out the answer to 4 x 600 x 25 in ten seconds or less.

Tell how you would multiply 9 x 99 in your head.

Explain how you can easily figure out the answer to $10.00 - $7.99.

Explain how Yolanda came up with the answer to the following problem in five seconds: The total cost of six pairs of socks at $3.99 each, is $23.94.

Your teacher asks you to find the answer to 141 x 3. Tell why you selected one of the methods listed below.

141 × 3

1. Mental math

2. Paper and pencil

3. Calculator

Today is Monday, October 5th. How would you figure out what day of the week October 23 falls on?

OCTOBER

4	5	6	7	8	9	10
11	12	13	14	15	16	17
18	19	20	21	22	23	
25	26	27	28	29	30	31

Tell about a math shortcut you use.

What numbers can you compute in your head more quickly than you can figure out on a calculator or computer?

Your teacher tells you that you have 45 minutes to finish the science test. It is 10:06 now. Explain how you would figure the time when the test ends.

It is 8:00 am now. How would you determine the time 7 hours from now?

Estimation

List five words that mean *to estimate*.

What activities can you complete in just one minute's time?

How can you estimate the number of words on one page of a particular book? What procedures would you use?

Estimate how many M & M's are in a small package. How did you come up with your answer? How close was your estimate to the actual number of M & M's?

Ten inches of snow equal one inch of rain. Over 31 inches of snow came down one night. How do you know at a glance that more than 3 inches of rain fell?

Estimate the number of marbles contained in a very large fish bowl. Why doesn't it matter if you over or underestimate the total number of marbles by 100?

A school is having a contest on estimating the number of jelly beans in a large jar. Tell how you would go about estimating the number of jelly beans.

Find examples in the newspaper where estimated numbers are used. Explain why you think estimated numbers were chosen over exact answers.

Under what circumstances are estimated answers better than exact answers?

Allison has $.60. She bought a bag of potato chips. How much money did she have left? Which answer is the most reasonable of the following choices? Why?

1. $ .60
2. $ .20
3. $1.00

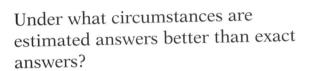

An estimated answer to 362 + 497 is 900. Tell how you know that the estimated answer is an underestimate or an overestimate.

In estimating the answer to 406 x 819, how do you know that an estimate of 320,000 is an underestimate?

What pairs of numbers below add up to more than 1000? Explain how you know.

638	369	153
421	511	286
712	211	198

Take a small container and fill it with a variety of coins. Record your estimate of how much money is in the container. Then, count the money. How close were you? Finally, tell how you went about counting the money. Did you make piles of one dollar or did you try to keep the total in your head? Did you make any mistakes and have to start over? How should someone go about counting a container of money?

Problem Solving

Write a story problem that contains too much information.

Write a story problem that has too little information.

Write a story problem and leave out the question.

Write a story that ends with a question. The question can be answered by any one of the following words: addition, multiplication, subtraction, or division.

Write a question to a problem. Then ask someone else to write the problem. For example,

Question: How many more horseshoes did Ross own than Mark?

Problem: Mark Decker and Ross Dilibert have a collection of horseshoes. Mark has 67 in his collection and Ross has 109.

Carl remembered that the answer to yesterday's board problem was 48, but he couldn't remember what the problem was. Help Carl by writing a story problem with an answer of 48.

Write a problem without using numbers. Leave the numbers for someone else to fill in.

Read the following numbers: $2.98, 4, 12, $16.75. Then write a story problem using some or all of the numbers.

Cut a picture out of a magazine. Then write a story problem based on your picture.

Write a story problem that involves oranges, bananas, or some other fruit. Make your fruit come to life. For example: There are six oranges swimming in a pool. After doing seven laps each, they....

Include your favorite musical group in a story problem.

Write a math problem using your favorite cartoon character.

Use your favorite television character in a story problem.

Invent an imaginary character and give it a name. It can be either a person or an animal. Then include your character in a math problem. For example:

▶ Jeremy, the giraffe...

▶ Mr. Pickersnurd, the rich old ...

▶ Benny, the boa...

▶ Mrs. Treebrook, the nursery owner...

▶ Alice, the alligator...

▶ Ms. Pool, the swimming instructor...

▶ Mrs. Keys, the piano teacher...

▶ Ms. Motor, the auto mechanic...

Take a word problem from your math book and rewrite it in your own words.

Explain how subtraction is the opposite of addition.

Write story problems based on various holidays, such as Halloween, New Year's Day, and Flag Day.

If you add 2 + 2 to get 4, and 4 + 4 to get 8, and 8 + 8 to get 16, how many additions would you have to do to get a 5-digit number as your answer? First, take a guess at the number of additions needed. Next, do the additions. Last, tell the number of actual additions that were needed and how close your estimate was. Oh, by the way, what answer did you get?

Suppose you didn't know how to add. Explain how you would find the answer to the following problem: Joan made 4 apple pies for Thanksgiving dinner. She also made 6 more pies for the homeless shelter. How many apple pies did she make in all?

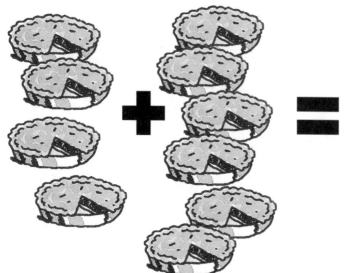

Tucker, the Golden Retriever, had 8 bones in his food dish. He ate 6 bones. Suppose you didn't know anything about subtraction. How would you figure out how many bones he had left?

Book Link

Read *Alexander, Who Used to be Rich Last Sunday*, by Judith Viorst. Explain how you found out how much money Alexander has at the end of the story.

Explain how you figured out the missing digits in the example below.

$$
\begin{array}{r}
6\,4\,\square \\
-\ \square\,\square\,7 \\
\hline
2\,8\,9
\end{array}
$$

Sylvia has completed four pages in her Mexican stamp book. Each page has four stamps. Suppose Sylvia does not know how to multiply. Describe three different ways she can figure out how many stamps she has collected so far.

Rachel won the Stamp Club contest for having the most stamps with 275. Explain why neither Nathan nor Megan won the stamp collecting contest. Nathan had 25 pages filled with 10 stamps per page, and Megan had 10 pages filled with 25 stamps per page.

Tina is a smart shopper. How does she know that buying 6 items for $1.00 is more economical than buying 6 items for 20 cents each?

Which is a better deal for Timothy Jones: receiving a check for $1,000 per month for one year or receiving 1 cent for the first day, 2 cents for the second day, and doubling that amount each day for one month's time? Explain your answer.

Tell how you figure out the missing number in $3 \times 3 \times$ ___ $= 36$.

The Lee family wanted to have a pizza delivered to their home. When the delivery person came to the door, no one in the family had any money to pay for the pizza. Tell where in the house family members might look to find enough loose change to pay for the pizza.

If you add three consecutive numbers, explain why you arrive at the same answer by multiplying the middle number by 3.

Explain why this trick works.

Take a number......842
Multiply by 10......8420
Subtract 842......7578
Divide by 9......842

Explain how division is the opposite of multiplication.

Kim is having 8 of her friends over for lunch. She has 24 cookies to serve. If each of her friends receives an equal number of cookies, how many cookies can each person have? Explain how you would arrive at your answer. Assume that you do not know how to divide.

Book Link

Read *Pigs Will Be Pigs*, by Amy Axelrod. Describe how you found out how much money the family was able to put together for dinner.

Joan and Tom worked together to present this problem to the class: Tennis balls are sold 3 to a container. Twenty-two balls are needed for field day events. How many cans of balls are needed? Explain your answer.

If one box contains 300 tissues, how do you figure out how many boxes to buy if you need 1,000 tissues?

Maria's Pizzeria puts 48 pieces of pepperoni on the pizzas she sells, and Salvatore's Pizzeria puts 24 pieces on the pizzas he sells. Yet, they both use one roll of the same kind of pepperoni. How could that be?

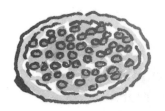
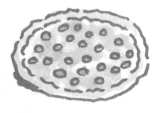

The Smith family has three children and a dog. The Jones family has four children and a cat. Each family had an uncle who left the children a total of $1,200. Who will inherit the most money—the Smith or the Jones children? How do you know?

Look at the containers below. Fill each one with the correct amount of money. Describe the number and denomination of each coin you used. Could you have used fewer coins in each container? Explain.

If a light were ON, would it still be on after four clicks? Seven clicks? How do you know? What happens with an even number of clicks?

Is it possible to have 2 fathers and 2 cousins in the same room if there are only 3 people there? Explain your answer.

You throw four darts to score exactly 100 points. You can hit the same number more than once. Which number makes it impossible to score 100 with just four darts? How do you know?

A wise mother was asked by her son if he could cut a candy bar and give part of it to his little sister. The mother, wanting to be fair, instructed the older child to cut the candy bar into 2 pieces and to allow the younger child to choose first. Why was the mother wise to do this?

Explain how you know what your age will be in the year 2000.

Haley is very clever when it comes to math. For homework, she has ten problems to do. Each problem involves putting three numbers in order, from lowest to highest. When she got to school, Mr. Juan, her math teacher, started to read all three numbers for each example. Haley raised her hand. All he had to do, she said, was read the lowest and the highest numbers. Why? Is there another pair of numbers Mr. Juan could have read?

Why is it faster to count to 500 by 25s than by 10s?

Tell why a person counting by 10 would reach 200 faster than a person counting by 5s.

Marianne says that when she needs to work with fraction pieces, she prefers circles rather than rectangles. Why do you think this is so?

Your littler brother or sister says that a nickel is worth more than a dime because a nickel is larger. What would you say to explain the value of each coin?

Larry said that three dimes are worth more than two quarters because 3 is greater than 2. What's wrong with his reasoning?

Under what circumstances would a shopper not be bothered if the price of an item increased by 100 percent?

Joe is a good shopper. One store sells tomato soup for 20 cents a can. Another store sells two cans of the same brand for 39 cents. If Joe buys only one can of tomato soup, does it matter which store he shops at? Why?

Patty spent $3.98 for a new hat. The clerk gave her $7.02 change from a $10.00 bill. Is the change correct? How do you know?

There are five people in a room. How many hands are there? Fingers? Eyes? Arms? Toes? How did you figure out each?

There are five people in a room. They all are introduced to each other and they all shake hands. Describe how you would figure out the total number of handshakes.

Select a stock and observe its price for one week. Pretend that you could buy 120 shares of the stock on Monday but had to sell it on Friday. Tell the class what you learned about the stock and whether you would have made or lost any money.

Write a story problem using the road sign below.

Part 2

Math Outside of School

What time is it? Do I have my lunch money? I wonder how well the Red Wings will score today? Do away with the one dollar bill? Females live longer than males? From the time students wake up in the morning to the time they arrive at school, they have already come across numerous math ideas articulated by family and friends, radio, television news, and newspapers. Writing about math outside of school not only helps students to see purpose in studying math as a subject but also provides an opportunity to apply and reinforce school learning. Students are unconsciously thinking about math as they carry on their daily routines and responsibilities. Many earn and spend money, and interact with family members in mathematical ways. Their sports, games, and hobbies also reflect mathematical interactions. Reflecting on the many uses of math helps

Family

List the names of your family members from the oldest to the youngest. Then, write a sentence that tells something about each one. Oh, don't forget your family pet(s)!

List the names of your family members by height. You may start with the tallest or the shortest first.

A girl is 13 years old. Her father is 1 more than 3 times her age. Explain how you would figure out her father's age.

Make a list of the birthdays of people who are important to you. Arrange them chronologically.

Write a story problem using one of your parents, your brother, your sister, or a pet.

Explain to a younger brother or sister why math is important.

Look around your kitchen. Count the number of glasses, cups, forks, spoons, knives, and dinner plates. Make a chart. Then write about what you have the most or the least of.

How much money do you think your parents spend on food every week? Check with them and compare your estimate with the actual amount they spend. Any surprises?

What would you serve a family of four for dinner if you had only $10 to spend for the entire meal?

How does your family spend its money?

Todd's grandfather was born in January of 1941. If it is June of 1998, explain how you would figure out the grandfather's age.

Saving, Spending, and Selling

On what do you spend your allowance?

On what do you think other kids spend their money?.

Do you think kids should have to work to earn an allowance? Explain your answer.

List several ways kids can earn money.

Patty needs $56.00 to buy school clothes. Suggest four ways that she can earn the money.

What store coupons does your family use?

What's the purpose of using coupons when you shop at the supermarket?

Do you think that coupons save consumers money or that they are more trouble than they are worth?

What purchases have you made lately?

How often do you compare prices when shopping?

Why do stores have sales?

Why are some sales really not sales at all?

Why do stores often sell items for $5.99 instead of $6.00?

Describe two ways that stores try to encourage consumers to spend money.

How do advertisers try to encourage consumers to buy their products? Tell whether you think consumers should pay attention to advertising.

If you owned a store or business what would you do to attract more customers?

Write an ad for an item you would like to sell.

If you wanted to buy this bicycle, what questions would you ask the seller?

Using the automobile ads in your local newspaper, tell what makes and features you can expect from an automobile selling for $5,000 or less.

Using the newspaper, look at store ads promoting televisions. Then compare the cost of two different TVs. Why do the prices differ? Are there special features? In your opinion which one would be a better buy?

List the zip codes for your hometown and for five surrounding towns. Do you notice anything in common about the numbers? What?

What did you do today that required you to use math?

Select six numbers for the lottery. Why did you pick those particular numbers?

Did someone ever give you the wrong change? Explain what happened.

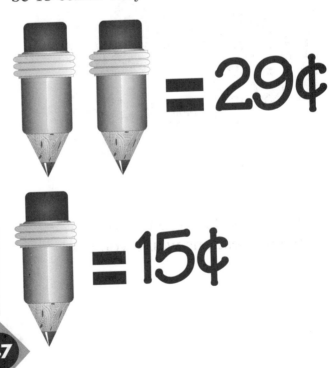

In a certain store, two pencils are selling for 29 cents. If you wanted to buy just one pencil, the cost would be 15 cents. Why?

Look at a product label on a can or box. What do all the numbers mean?

Explain which is a better buy: two 24–ounce boxes of cereal for $.96 or three 20–ounce boxes of the same cereal for $1.20.

Why is it more economical to purchase 3 items for $1.00 than to purchase each item for 35 cents?

What does it mean to pay an 8% sales tax on a $12.00 purchase?

Sports, Hobbies, and Games

Explain how to keep score in bowling.

Why is it useful for ball players to have numbers on their jerseys? List your favorite ball players and their jersey numbers.

Predict the score for your favorite football team and its opponent. Why did you predict that score?

How is math used in sports?

How is math used in your favorite sport?

What salary is your favorite sports hero worth? Why?

Why can coin collecting be a profitable hobby? What kinds of things do you need to think about when collecting coins?

Read about a trick done with numbers. Then, write your own set of directions explaining the trick.

Explain a math game you know how to play.

What's your favorite game that involves making use of numbers?

Opinions

Three sixth graders formed a singing group called the Three Lightbulbs. (They wanted to light up people's lives!) They were so good that they were offered a record contract with RAY Record Company. What kinds of things do you think should go into their contract?

"I just traded a dollar bill for 2 fifty cent pieces," says Barny. "Then I traded them in for 4 quarters. As anyone can tell you, I'm richer now because I have more money than when I started. Four is more than one!" Does Barny actually have more money? Where did he go wrong in his thinking?

What effect would a higher tax on cigarettes and alcohol have on these products?

The state lottery prize was $7,000,000. You need six numbers to play the lottery. What six numbers would you choose? Do these numbers have any special meaning to you? What do you think your chances of winning are?

How tall will you be when you are 21 years old? Why do you think you'll be that tall?

People in the United States write the date as 9/23/97. In Europe, they write the same date as 23/9/97. Which way do you think is better? Why?

Should there only be a coin with a value of $1.00 or should we keep the dollar bill? Explain your answer.

Some Americans say we should do away with the penny. What do you think? Why?

The life expectancy of females is greater than that of males. Why do you think this is true?

Why do the governors of most states have a license plate with only the number 1 on it?

Tell whether you believe waiters, waitresses, and other service people should receive tips. Explain your answer.

How much money should you tip a waitress? What factors would you consider in your decision?

What factors would you consider in figuring out how much you would charge for babysitting?

Why do convenience stores charge more than supermarkets for the same products?

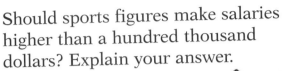

Should sports figures make salaries higher than a hundred thousand dollars? Explain your answer.

Name five occupations. Then list them in order of the salary you think they deserve—from highest to lowest. Tell why you ranked each the way you did.

Why do you need to study math?

Someone once said that math students are born not made. What do you think?

Marie's brother claims that he is not good in math. What advice should Marie give him?

Who would hire a mathematician?

Julia is in sixth grade. She says that all regular watches should be thrown out and only digital watches be used. What do you think about Julia's idea?

Part 3

Math and Language Arts

Regardless of where or when writing skills are taught during the school day, elementary classroom teachers are constantly thinking about how to teach the prescribed Language Arts curriculum. In almost any school, teachers can be heard saying:

"Students need different kinds of writing."

"Our curriculum says that I have to teach letter writing."

"Poetry is a favorite topic of mine."

"We have to cover literature and writing reviews."

"It's important for students to publish their written work."

"We need to write two creative stories per week."

All of the above and more can be accomplished during the Language Arts period using math as the content. Here is where math can be used to teach writing.

Poetry

Choose a favorite number and write a poem about it. For example, write a poem about the number 7:

Lucky seven
You came from heaven.
I win a lot
Because I pick you a lot!

Write a poem about the number 10.

Number 10 you are my friend.
You're the living end.
Three times 10 I know
Ten times 10 I know.
25 times 10 I know, too.
Thanks to you!

Write a poem or little song about the months of the year or the days of the week. For example:

Fridays, Fridays,
The best day of the week.
Payday, fun day, weekend treats!

Have discussions about individual poems for their mathematical content. Have students describe what happened in each poem. As extensions, students can:

▶ Write their reactions to the poem.

▶ Write their own poem using the ones they read as a model.

Book Link

Investigate the poetry of Shel Silverstein.

In *Where the Sidewalk Ends*, read the following poems:

▶ "Smart"
▶ "The Googies Are Coming"
▶ "Eighteen Flavors"
▶ "Band-Aids"
▶ "Hungry Mungry"

In *A Light in the Attic*, read the following poem:

▶ "Overdues"

Now select one of the Silverstein poems that you just read and answer the questions below.

▶ Tell what numbers were in the poem.
▶ What does math have to do with the poem?
▶ Write a story problem based on the poem.
▶ Write your own math poem. Use one of the poems as a model.
▶ Make up your own math-related questions.

Book Link

Read the following poems from Jack Prelutsky's *The New Kid on the Block:*

▶ "Bleezer's Ice Cream"
▶ "Baloney Belly Billy"

What do these poems have to do with math?

Write riddles such as:

One half of me is 13. Who am I?

If you add 4 to twice me, you would get 4? Who am I?

I am the same as 1/2 dozen. Who am I?

Write a math rhyme. For example:

▶ Fractions are great
But decimals really rate.

▶ I am odd, will you get even?

▶ Problems! Problems! Problems! I don't have a problem with problems.

▶ Does a goose have a hypotenuse?

▶ I add money to my account. I never want to take it out.

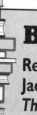

▶ There is the prime of your life,
The prime suspect, and
The prime rib.
But, best of all, are prime numbers.

Figuring out my number friends is easy. Guess who they are.

▶ I was 100 but now I am 60 less.
Who am I?_____

▶ You would know me if you know 50 + 25 + 10 + 5 + 10.
Who am I?

▶ One-half of me is 500.
Who am I?

▶ If you square the number of days in a week, you'll know me. Who am I?

▶ I'm odd, over 50, and double digits.
Who am I?

▶ My maiden name is 3^2. I married 4^2. My new name is the sum of our two names.
Who am I?

Write your own *Who am I* riddle!

Write a math riddle or joke. Before you start, read the following examples:

What number often goes to the hospital because of illness?
Answer: Sickteen!

What is the difference between 30 and 20?
Answer: 10!

Do you know what number speaks German?
Answer: Nine!

After reading poems involving various math themes, suggest several ideas to students so they can write their own poems. Topics may include money, time, metrics, shopping, and allowance.

Choose a math topic you have studied. Write a short poem about it.

Write a math rap. For example:

Doing fractions gives satisfaction. Knowing your numerator lets you know your denominator. Keep your denominator common and you'll have no problem.

Design a math bumper sticker. For example:

GEOMETRY COMES IN ALL SHAPES!

FRACTIONS THINK SMALL

TAKE A CHANCE. STUDY PROBABILITY!

MATH MAKES | THINGS ADD UP!

SOME NUMBERS ARE SQUARE!

SOME NUMBERS ARE PERFECT!

Write number or math graffiti. The following examples should give you some ideas:

▶ H-m-m, what's next?
100, 93, 86, _____?
Tina

▶ T.J.'s phone number is 2-8-1-apple!
Karen

▶ Get a life! Study math! Get a job!
Tim

▶ 9-23-88 is a special date for me.
Thomas

▶ I like making graphs!
T.J.

▶ Symmetrical and hypothetical are mathematical.
Bette Sue

After reading the following examples, write sentences in which math words are used humorously. Then use your sentences to create T-shirt designs.

▶ **Statistics are numbered!**

▶ **Fractions break me up!**

▶ **Metric users really measure up!**

▶ **Circumference keeps me going in circles!**

▶ **Scales? What a heavy thought!**

▶ **Decimals are for small thinkers.**

▶ **Math lights up my life.**

Write a math jingle to a famous tune.
For example: To the tune *Mary Had a Little Lamb*—

Geometry is about lines and shapes, lines and shapes, lines and shapes.

Creative Writing

Write a script for a video. You may tell how to:

▶ solve a problem
▶ explain a math idea
▶ teach an up-coming math topic

Write a creative story using any of the titles below.

How It Came To Be and Other Tales: The Day Division Was Invented

Why Multiplication Was Invented

How Numbers Became Squares

Six Did Not Pick Up Sticks

The Prime Minister of Numbers

How I Became a Roman Numeral

How I Became an Odd Number

How I Made a Million in the Stock Market

Write a story in which the characters, people, and events are all math words. For example: Mr. Peri Meter met Mr. E.Z. Math on the corner of Geometry Street and Angle Avenue. They were going to lunch at the Square Deal Restaurant.

When I arrived at school, there was Tucker showing off his three new pencils. Then I went to my desk and got my seven pencils to sharpen. Tucker and I were talking loudly about who was first in line to sharpen pencils. Finally, my teacher, Mr. Zuk, asked us to please lower our voices. Then we sharpened our pencils. How many pencils did we sharpen all together?

Four trick-or-treaters are lined up in front of a house waiting for candy. Superman is not first in line. The clown is last and next to her is Cinderella. Batman is also waiting. Tell how the four characters are lined up. Now write a similar logic problem. If you need to, make a drawing to help you.

Describe what you might find in the make-believe place called Number-land.

Make a rhyme in the following way:

6 and 8 went on a date
6 x 8 is 48.

6 and 7 lost their shoe
6 x 7 is 42.

6 and 9 washed the floor
6 x 9 is 54.

Use the number sentence 3 + 7 = 10 to write a story. Use the guide below:

When I arrived at school...
Then I ...
Finally my teacher...

Try writing a fairy tale to include numerical information. For example, read this version of *The Three Little Pigs:*

Once upon a time there were three little pigs. The oldest was Buffa. He was 14 years old and he liked to tell jokes. Next came Herbert who was 12 years old. He was the funniest of the three, etc...

Include numerical information for several cartoon characters. For example: Donald Duck's three nephews are Louie, Dewey, and Huey. How old is each one? How tall? What are their favorite numbers? When are their birthdays?

Design your own restaurant menu. Name the restaurant after yourself. Select items to be placed on the menu and be sure to include prices. Write a description of what your restaurant would look like.

Design a product and write an advertisement to promote its sale. Be sure to describe your product and determine a price. Explain why your product is worth the price you are charging.

Make up a saying to help you remember those months of the year that have 30 days.

What is the recipe for your favorite food?

Create a recipe for making your favorite kind of pizza.

Write a set of directions on how to fold a sheet of paper so that when the paper is unfolded, you have eight equal parts.

Someone rings your doorbell and asks for a $10 donation. What would you do?

Write a short biography about a famous mathematician.

Who was Fibonacci?

Who was Benjamin Banneker?

Research and write about a famous female mathematician.

Who is Sonya Kovalevsky?

Write your mathematical autobiography. Tell about your successes and failures. Also, tell how numbers have played an important part in your life.

Listen to the evening news. What was in the news that required the use of mathematics?

Interview your school district's superintendent. Ask him or her about such things as:

1. The number of pupils in the district
2. Total school budget
3. Cost per pupil
4. Average teacher's salary

Make up some other questions. Report this information in your school newspaper.

Arrange an interview with the school nurse. Find out how she uses math in her daily work. Consider publishing your interview in the school newspaper.

Write a story problem, riddle, or math brain teaser for your school or classroom paper. Ask for replies. Then write the names of everyone who correctly solved the riddle in the next issue of the paper.

Write a letter to the publishers of your math book. Tell them what you like and dislike about their math book.

Look through your math book. Then write a page-long book review. Using the front page of the newspaper, circle all words, symbols, and ideas that relate to numbers. Were you surprised by the different ways in which numbers were used? Explain.

Interview an adult and report how they use numbers or number ideas in their work.